THE
WORDS
OF
CHRIST

"I am come that they might
have life, and that they
might have it more
abundantly."

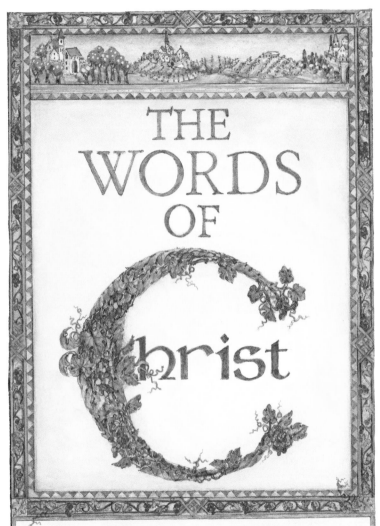

THE WORDS OF Christ

An Illuminated Volume
By Judy Pelikan

FaithWords
Hachette Book Group
1290 Avenue of the Americas, New York, NY 10104
faithwords.com
twitter.com/faithwords

First Edition: September 2018

FaithWords is a division of Hachette Book Group, Inc. The
FaithWords name and logo are trademarks of Hachette Book
Group, Inc.

Editor: Adrienne Ingrum
Typesetting: Margery Cantor
Jacket Design by Judy Pelikan

Excerpts from *The Four Gospels and The Revelation,* translated
from the Greek by Richmond Lattimore. Copyright 1962, 1979
by Richmond Lattimore.
Reprinted by permission of Farrar, Straus and Giroux, Inc.
Scripture quotations taken from the New American Standard
Bible® (NASB),
Copyright © 1960, 1962, 1963, 1968, 1971, 1972, 1973,
1975, 1977, 1995 by The Lockman Foundation
Used by permission. www.Lockman.org
ISBN: 978-1-5460-3193-2
Printed in the United States of America / WOR

10 9 8 7 6 5 4 3 2 1

As the branch cannot bear fruit of itself, except it abide in the vine; no more can ye, except ye abide in me. I am the vine, ye are the branches."

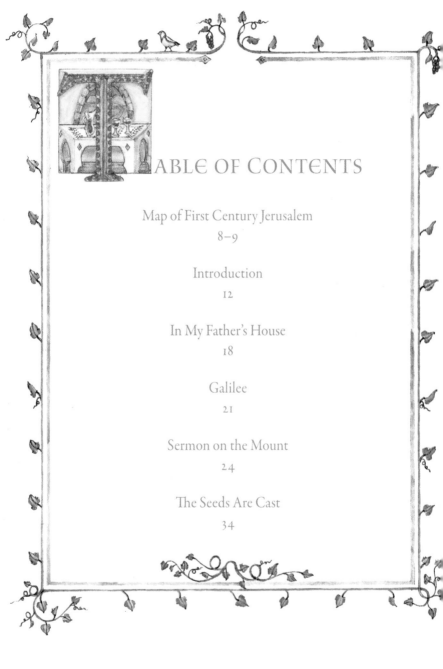

TABLE OF CONTENTS

INTRODUCTION

What was it that Jesus wanted us to know? What was the essence of the gift he brought to us, the intrinsic nature of his teachings that has nourished humanity for thousands of years?

The influence of the words of Christ down the centuries has touched and transformed so many lives. Charles Dickens, the most famous English author of the 19th century, gave his son, when he was leaving home, a copy of the New Testament, with a note "It is the best book that ever was or will be known in this world."

In a letter to his notable political rival and friend John Adams, Thomas Jefferson wrote that in the words

of Jesus, "There will be found . . . the most sublime and benevolent code of morals which has ever been offered to man."

Leo Tolstoy, the giant of Russian literature, offered that the words of Christ expressed "the only doctrine that gives meaning to life."

Certainly today we are in need of Christ's teaching, his wisdom and his words. A sage friend expressed the reason so eloquently: "Because despair is around every corner, there is a great need to reflect on Jesus's words. Through the ages his words have soothed us and opened our hearts. They have given us direction to work for justice and to love."

Years ago Anne Van Rensselaer and I were eager to cull from the New Testament the essential teachings and inherent wisdom in Jesus's words, without commentary. Our aim was to weave them together in a compelling and visually stunning book, a book to physically embody the beauty contained within.

We were fortunate that Judy Pelikan, an artist of deep faith as well as talent, honored us with her luminous watercolors. Taking advantage of the poetry of the King James edition and a few other translations, we shaped text and images into *The Words of Christ: An Illuminated Volume,* and in 1986 an edition, a large format version was published.

For this smaller edition of *The Words of Christ,* we were again blessed to work with Judy Pelikan, who over the years has honed her craft well beyond our initial version. As a serious student of the New Testament she has deepened her knowledge of the flora and fauna of the Holy Land. Each of her books exhibits her humanity and expresses her faith as well as her skill. And never before have her illustrations so beautifully reflected the Holy Land's landscape and wild-life, the land Jesus knew.

As we immersed ourselves in the words of Christ, we were humbled by their simplicity and clarity of intent. Jesus teaches that everyone is formed of Spirit

by the Divine Creator. To know this is to dignify each and every human being, whether homeless, victims of discrimination, or born to privilege. He reminds us that "Unto whom is given much, much is required." And Jesus tells us that, "Ye shall know them by their fruits. Do men gather grapes of thorns, or figs of thistles? Even so every good tree bringeth forth good fruit: but a corrupt tree bringeth forth evil fruit ... Where for by their fruits ye shall know them."

If we have "ears to hear" his words, we will care and comfort the sick, practice justice not hypocrisy and corruption, serve the disenfranchised, feed the hungry and walk humbly with God. The life Jesus illuminates is available to all and manifests through our acts of love toward one another. The love Jesus expresses in his words—and demonstrated in his life—is the compass on our spiritual journey.

We need to be reminded of Christ's words. His compassion, empathy and healing words are needed today. The "Good News" of the words of Jesus in the New Testament is that if we but practice them, our lives and our world can be transformed. "For behold, the kingdom of God is in your midst." "The Kingdom of God is within you." "Thy Kingdom Come!"

It is our wish that this small edition will bring you a powerful measure of comfort, inspiration and hope. Take it with you and you will not walk alone.

Jane Lahr & Anne Van Rensselaer

* This volume primarily comprises the teachings of Jesus, his words. Because of that fact, in this edition, unlike some New Testaments, we have set the text from the Old Testament that Jesus incorporated into his teaching in red.

t is written,
Man shall not
live by bread alone,
but by every word
that proceedeth out of
the mouth of God."

hen Jesus was twelve years old, his parents took him to Jerusalem for the feast of Passover. While his parents were returning home, the child had tarried behind. After searching for him for three days they found him in the temple sitting in the midst of the teachers, listening to them and asking them questions. And his mother said to him, "Son, why have you treated us this way?" And he said to them, "But why were you looking for me? Did you not know that I must be in my father's house?"

hen Jesus was about thirty years of age, he was led by the Spirit into the wilderness to be tempted by the devil. After fasting forty days and forty nights, he was hungry. The tempter came to him and said, "If thou be the Son of God, command that these stones be made bread." Jesus answered and said,

t is written, Man shall not live by bread alone, but by every word that proceedeth out of the mouth of God."

Then the devil took him to the holy city and had him stand on the highest point of the temple. "If thou be the Son of God, cast thyself down, for it is written, He shall give his angels charge concerning thee, and in their hands they shall bear thee up, lest at any time thou dash thy foot against a stone." Jesus answered him, "It is written again, Thou shalt not tempt the Lord thy God."

Again, the devil took him up into a very high mountain, and showed him all the kingdoms of the world and all their splendor. "All these things will I give thee, if thou wilt fall down and worship me."

Then Jesus answered him, "Get thee hence, Satan, for it is written, Thou shalt worship the Lord thy God, and him only shalt thou serve."

When Passover was at hand, Jesus went up to Jerusalem, and found there those that sold oxen and sheep and doves, and the changers of money. And he made a scourge and drove them all out of the temple, with the sheep and the oxen; and he poured out the coins of the moneychangers, and overturned their tables; and said unto them, "Take these things away; stop making my Father's house a house of merchandise."

of the Lord is upon me, because He anointed me
to preach the gospel to the poor. He has sent me to
proclaim release to the captives, and recovery of sight
to the blind, to set free those who are downtrodden,
to proclaim the favorable year of the Lord."

Now there was a man of the Pharisees, named Nicodemus, a ruler of the Jews; this man came to him by night, and said to him, "Rabbi, we know that you have come from God as a teacher; for one cannot do these signs that you do unless God is with him." Jesus answered and said to him, "Truly, truly, I say to you, unless one is born again, he cannot see the kingdom of God." Nicodemus said to him, "How can a man be born when he is old? He cannot enter a second time into his mother's womb and be born, can he?" Jesus answered, "Truly, truly, I say to you, unless one is born of water and the Spirit he cannot enter into the Kingdom of God. That which is born of the flesh is flesh, and that which is born of the Spirit is spirit. Do not marvel that I said to you, 'You must be born again.' The wind blows where it wishes and you hear the sound of it, but do not know where it comes from and where it is going; so is everyone who is born of the Spirit."

Nicodemus said to him, "How can these things be?"

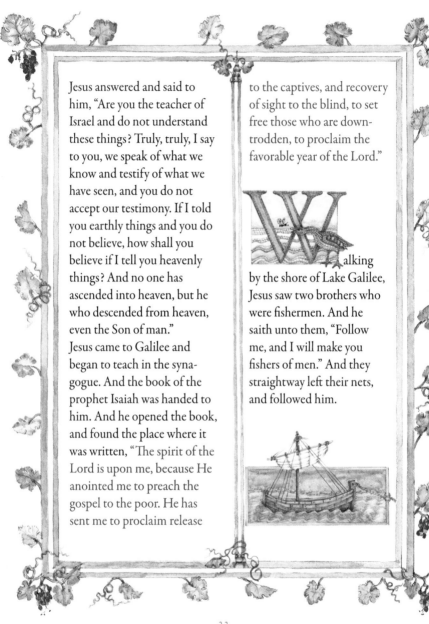

Jesus answered and said to him, "Are you the teacher of Israel and do not understand these things? Truly, truly, I say to you, we speak of what we know and testify of what we have seen, and you do not accept our testimony. If I told you earthly things and you do not believe, how shall you believe if I tell you heavenly things? And no one has ascended into heaven, but he who descended from heaven, even the Son of man."

Jesus came to Galilee and began to teach in the synagogue. And the book of the prophet Isaiah was handed to him. And he opened the book, and found the place where it was written, "The spirit of the Lord is upon me, because He anointed me to preach the gospel to the poor. He has sent me to proclaim release to the captives, and recovery of sight to the blind, to set free those who are downtrodden, to proclaim the favorable year of the Lord."

Walking by the shore of Lake Galilee, Jesus saw two brothers who were fishermen. And he saith unto them, "Follow me, and I will make you fishers of men." And they straightway left their nets, and followed him.

DO not give
what is holy to dogs, and
do not throw your pearls
before swine, lest they tramp
them under their feet, and
turn and tear you to pieces.

**A**nd seeing the multitudes, he went up into a mountain; and when he was set, his disciples came unto him: and he opened his mouth, and taught them, saying, "Blessed are the poor in spirit: for theirs is the kingdom of heaven. Blessed are they that mourn: for they shall be comforted. Blessed are the meek: for they shall inherit the earth. Blessed are they which do hunger and thirst after righteousness: for they shall be filled. Blessed are the merciful: for they shall obtain mercy. Blessed are the pure in heart: for they shall see God.

Blessed are the peacemakers: for they shall be called the children of God. Blessed are they which are persecuted for righteousness' sake: for theirs is the kingdom of heaven.

BLESSED are ye, when men shall revile you, and persecute you, and shall say all manner of evil against you falsely, for my sake. Rejoice, and be exceeding glad; for great is your reward in heaven; for so persecuted they the prophets which were before you.

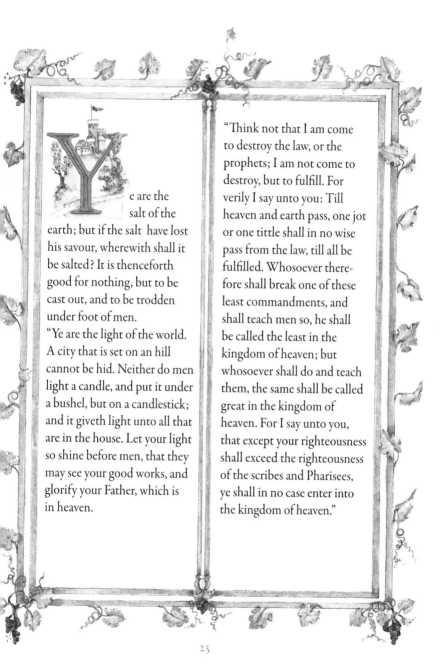

Ye are the salt of the earth; but if the salt have lost his savour, wherewith shall it be salted? It is thenceforth good for nothing, but to be cast out, and to be trodden under foot of men.

"Ye are the light of the world. A city that is set on an hill cannot be hid. Neither do men light a candle, and put it under a bushel, but on a candlestick; and it giveth light unto all that are in the house. Let your light so shine before men, that they may see your good works, and glorify your Father, which is in heaven.

"Think not that I am come to destroy the law, or the prophets; I am not come to destroy, but to fulfill. For verily I say unto you: Till heaven and earth pass, one jot or one tittle shall in no wise pass from the law, till all be fulfilled. Whosoever therefore shall break one of these least commandments, and shall teach men so, he shall be called the least in the kingdom of heaven; but whosoever shall do and teach them, the same shall be called great in the kingdom of heaven. For I say unto you, that except your righteousness shall exceed the righteousness of the scribes and Pharisees, ye shall in no case enter into the kingdom of heaven."

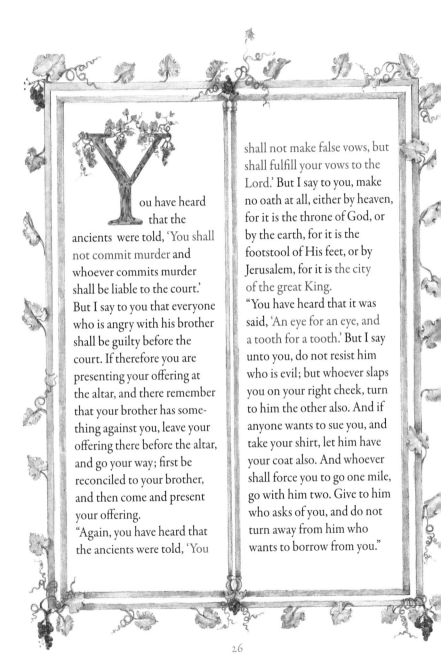

You have heard that the ancients were told, 'You shall not commit murder and whoever commits murder shall be liable to the court.' But I say to you that everyone who is angry with his brother shall be guilty before the court. If therefore you are presenting your offering at the altar, and there remember that your brother has something against you, leave your offering there before the altar, and go your way; first be reconciled to your brother, and then come and present your offering.

"Again, you have heard that the ancients were told, 'You shall not make false vows, but shall fulfill your vows to the Lord.' But I say to you, make no oath at all, either by heaven, for it is the throne of God, or by the earth, for it is the footstool of His feet, or by Jerusalem, for it is the city of the great King.

"You have heard that it was said, 'An eye for an eye, and a tooth for a tooth.' But I say unto you, do not resist him who is evil; but whoever slaps you on your right cheek, turn to him the other also. And if anyone wants to sue you, and take your shirt, let him have your coat also. And whoever shall force you to go one mile, go with him two. Give to him who asks of you, and do not turn away from him who wants to borrow from you."

have heard that it hath been said, 'Thou shalt love thy neighbor, and hate thine enemy. But I say unto you: Love your enemies, bless them that curse you, do good to them that hate you, and pray for them which despitefully use you, and persecute you, that ye may be the children of your Father which is in heaven; for He maketh His sun to rise on the evil and on the good, and sendeth rain on the just and on the unjust. For if ye love them which love you, what reward have ye? Do not even the publicans the same? And if ye salute your brethren only, what do ye more than others?

Do not even the publicans so? Be ye therefore perfect, even as your Father which is in heaven is perfect.

"Give and it will be given to you; good measure, pressed down, shaken together, running over, they will pour into your lap. For by your standard of measure it will be measured to you in return."

Beware of practicing your righteousness before men to be noticed by them; otherwise you have no reward with your Father who is in heaven. "When therefore you give

sk, and it shall be given to you; seek, and you shall find; knock, and it shall be opened to you.

alms, do not sound a trumpet before you, as the hypocrites do in the synagogues and in the streets, that they may be honored by men. Truly I say to you, they have their reward in full. But when you give alms, do not let your left hand know what your right hand is doing, that your alms may be in secret; and your Father who sees in secret will repay you.

"And when you pray, you are not to be as the hypocrites; for they love to stand and pray in the synagogues and on the street corners, in order to be seen by men. Truly I say to you, they have their reward in full. But you, when you pray, go into your inner room, and when you have shut your door, pray to your Father who is in secret, and your Father who sees in secret will repay you.

And when you are praying, do not use meaningless repetition, as the Gentiles do, for they suppose that they will be heard for their many words. Therefore do not be like them, for your Father knows what you need before you ask Him."

ray, then in this way: Our Father who art in heaven, hallowed be Thy name. Thy kingdom come, Thy will be done, on earth as it is in heaven. Give us this day our daily bread. And forgive us our debts, as we also have forgiven our debtors. And do not lead us into temptation, but deliver us from evil. For Thine is the kingdom, and the power, and the glory, forever. Amen."

or if you forgive men for their transgressions, your heavenly Father will also forgive you. But if you do not forgive men, then your Father will not forgive your transgressions.

"And whenever you fast, do not put on a gloomy face as the hypocrites do, for they neglect their appearance in order to be seen fasting by men. Truly I say to you, they have their reward in full. But you, when you fast, anoint your head, and wash your face so that you may not be seen fasting by men, but by your Father who is in secret; and your Father who sees in secret will repay you."

"Do not lay up for yourselves treasures upon earth, where moth and rust destroy, and where thieves break in and steal. But lay up for yourselves treasures in heaven, where neither moth nor rust destroys, and where thieves do not break in or steal; for where your treasure is, there will your heart be also.

he light of the body is the eye: if therefore thine eye be single, thy whole body shall be full of light. But if thine eye be evil, thy whole

body shall be full of darkness! "No man can serve two masters: for either he will hate the one, and love the other; or else he will hold to the one, and despise the other. Ye cannot serve God and mammon. Therefore I say unto you, Take no thought for your life, what ye shall eat, or what ye shall drink; nor yet for your body, what ye shall put on. Is not the life more than meat, and the body than raiment? Behold the fowls of the air: for they sow not, neither do they reap, nor gather into barns; yet your heavenly Father feedeth them. Are ye not much better than they? Which of you by taking thought can add one cubit unto his stature?

And why take ye thought for raiment? Consider the lilies of the field, how they grow; they toil not, neither do they spin. And yet I say unto you, that even Solomon in all his glory was not arrayed like one of these. Wherefore, if God so clothe the grass of the field, which today is, and tomorrow is cast into the oven, shall He not much more clothe you, O ye of little faith? "Therefore take no thought, saying, 'What shall we eat?' or, 'What shall we drink?' or, 'Wherewithal shall we be clothed?' (For after all these things do the Gentiles seek.) For your heavenly Father knoweth that ye have need of all these things. But seek ye first the kingdom of God, and his righteousness; and all these things shall be added unto you. Take therefore no thought for the morrow, for the morrow shall take thought for the things of itself. Sufficient unto the day is the evil thereof.

o not judge lest you be judged. For in the way you judge, you will be judged; and by your standard of measure, it will be measured to you."

"Do not give what is holy to dogs, and do not throw your pearls before swine, lest they trample them under their feet, and turn and tear you to pieces."

sk, and it shall be given to you; seek, and you shall find; knock, and it shall be opened to you. For everyone who asks receives, and he who seeks finds, and to him who knocks it shall be opened. Or what man is there among you when his son shall ask him for a loaf will give him a stone? Or if he shall ask for a fish, he will not give him a snake, will he? If you then, being evil, know how to give good gifts to your children, how much more shall your Father who is in heaven give what is good to those who ask Him? Therefore, however you want people to treat you, so treat them, for this is the Law and the Prophets.

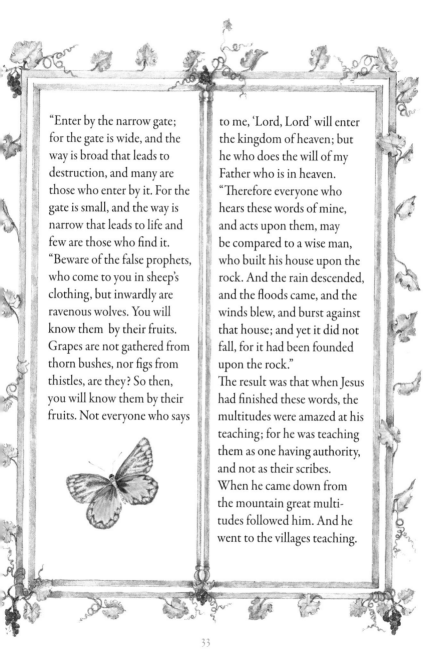

"Enter by the narrow gate; for the gate is wide, and the way is broad that leads to destruction, and many are those who enter by it. For the gate is small, and the way is narrow that leads to life and few are those who find it.

"Beware of the false prophets, who come to you in sheep's clothing, but inwardly are ravenous wolves. You will know them by their fruits. Grapes are not gathered from thorn bushes, nor figs from thistles, are they? So then, you will know them by their fruits. Not everyone who says to me, 'Lord, Lord' will enter the kingdom of heaven; but he who does the will of my Father who is in heaven.

"Therefore everyone who hears these words of mine, and acts upon them, may be compared to a wise man, who built his house upon the rock. And the rain descended, and the floods came, and the winds blew, and burst against that house; and yet it did not fall, for it had been founded upon the rock."

The result was that when Jesus had finished these words, the multitudes were amazed at his teaching; for he was teaching them as one having authority, and not as their scribes. When he came down from the mountain great multitudes followed him. And he went to the villages teaching.

ome to me, all who are weary and heavy-laden, and I will give you rest. Take my yoke upon you, and learn from me, for I am gentle and humble in heart; and you shall find rest for your souls. For my yoke is easy and my load is light."

aving summoned his twelve disciples, Jesus sent them out with these instructions: "Go not into the way of the Gentiles, and into any city of the Samaritans enter ye not. But go rather to the lost sheep of the house of Israel. And as ye go preach, saying, The kingdom of heaven is at hand. Heal the sick, cleanse the lepers, raise the dead, cast out devils; freely ye have received, freely give. Provide neither gold, nor silver, nor brass in your purses, nor scrip for your journey, neither two coats, neither shoes, nor yet staves, for the workman is worthy of his meat. And into whatsoever city or town ye shall enter, enquire who in it is worthy; and there abide till ye go thence. And when ye come into an house, salute it. And if the house be worthy, let your peace come upon it, but if it be not worthy, let your peace return to you. And whosoever shall not receive you, nor hear your words, when ye depart out of that house or city, shake off the dust of your feet."

ehold, I send you forth as sheep in the midst of wolves: be ye therefore wise as serpents, and harmless as doves. But beware of men, for they will deliver you up to the councils, and they will scourge you in their synagogues; and ye shall be brought before governors and kings for my sake, for a testimony against them and the Gentiles. "But when they deliver you up, take no thought how or what ye shall speak; for it shall be given you in that same hour what ye shall speak. For it is not ye that speak, but the Spirit of your Father which speaketh in you. "And the brother shall deliver up the brother to death, and the father the child, and the children shall rise up against their parents, and cause them to be put to death. And ye shall be hated of all men for my name's sake, but he that endureth to the end shall be saved. But when they persecute you in this city, flee ye into another, for verily I say unto you, Ye shall not have gone over the cities of Israel, till the Son of man be come."

disciple is not above his teacher, nor a slave above his master. It is enough for the disciple that he become as his teacher, and the slave as his master. If they have called the head of the house Beelzebub, how much more the members of his household! Therefore do not fear them, for there is nothing covered that will not be revealed, and hidden

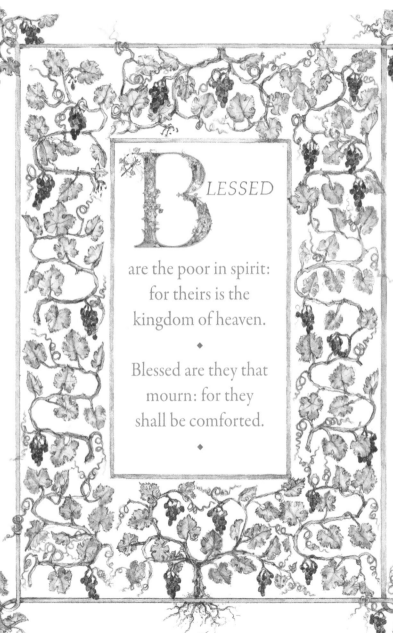

BLESSED

are the poor in spirit:
for theirs is the
kingdom of heaven.

◆

Blessed are they that
mourn: for they
shall be comforted.

◆

Blessed are the meek:
for they shall
inherit the earth.

◆

Blessed are they
which do hunger
and thirst after
righteousness: for
they shall be filled.

Blessed are
the merciful:
for they shall
obtain mercy.

◆

Blessed are the
pure in heart:
for they shall
see God.

◆

Blessed are
the peacemakers:
for they shall be called
the children of God.

◆

Blessed are they which
are persecuted for
righteousness sake:
for theirs is the
kingdom of heaven.

◆

Blessed are ye,
when men
shall revile you,
and persecute you,
and shall say all
manner of evil
against you falsely,
for my sake.

◆

REJOICE,

and be exceeding glad:
for great is your
reward in heaven:
for so persecuted they
the prophets which
were before you."

◆

that will not be known. What I tell you in the darkness, speak in the light; and what you hear whispered in your ear, proclaim upon the housetops.

And do not fear those who kill the body, but are unable to kill the soul; but rather fear Him who is able to destroy both soul and body in hell. Are not two sparrows sold for a cent? And yet not one of them will fall to the ground apart from your Father. But the very hairs of your head are all numbered. Therefore do not fear; you are of more value than many sparrows. Everyone therefore who shall confess me before men, I will also confess him before my Father who is in heaven. But whoever shall deny me before men, I will also deny him before my Father who is in heaven."

 o not think that I came to bring peace on the earth; I did not come to bring peace, but a sword. For I came to set a man against his father, and a daughter against her mother, and a daughter-in-law against her mother-in-law; and a man's enemies will be the members of his household. He who loves father or mother more than me is not worthy of me; and he who loves son or daughter more than me is not worthy of me. And he who does not take his cross and follow after me is not worthy of me. He who has found his life shall lose it, and he who has lost his life for my sake shall find it.

e who receives you receives me, and he who receives me receives Him who sent me. He who receives a prophet in the name of a prophet shall receive a prophet's reward; and he who receives a righteous man in the name of a righteous man shall receive a righteous man's reward."

nd he entered again into a synagogue; and a man was there with a withered hand. And they were watching him to see if he would heal him on the Sabbath, in order that they might accuse him. And he said to the man with the withered hand, "Rise and come forward!" And he said to them, "Is it lawful on the Sabbath to do good or to do harm, to save a life or to kill?" But they kept silent. And after looking around at them with anger, grieved at their hardness of heart, he said to the man, "Stretch out your hand." And he stretched it out, and his hand was restored. And the Pharisees went out and immediately began taking counsel with the Herodians against him, as to how they might destroy him.

hen told that his mother and his brothers wished to see him, he answered them, saying, "Who is my mother or my brethren?" And he looked round about on them which sat about him, and said, "Behold my mother and my brethren! For

drinking, and they say, 'He has a demon!' The Son of man came eating and drinking, and they say, 'Behold, a gluttonous man and a drunkard, a friend of tax-gatherers and sinners!' Yet wisdom is vindicated by her deeds."

whoever shall do the will of God, the same is my brother, and my sister, and mother."

And as these were going away, Jesus began to speak to the multitudes about John, "What did you go out into the wilderness to look at? A reed shaken by the wind? But what did you go out to see? A man dressed in soft clothing? Behold, those who wear soft clothing are in kings' palaces. This is the one about whom it is written, 'Behold, I send My messenger before your face, who will prepare your way before you.' And if you care to accept it, he himself is Elijah, who was to come. He who has ears to hear, let him hear. For John came neither eating nor

t that time Jesus went on the Sabbath through the grainfields, and his disciples became hungry and began to pick the heads of grain and eat. But when the Pharisees saw it, they said to him, "Behold, your disciples do what is not lawful to do on a Sabbath." But he said to them, "Have you not read what David did, when he became hungry, he and his companions; how he entered the house of God, and they ate the consecrated bread, which was not lawful for him to eat? Nor for those with him, but for the priests alone? Or have you not read in the Law, that on the Sabbath the priests in the temple break the Sabbath, and are innocent? But I say to you, that something greater than the temple is here. The Sabbath was made for man, and not man for the Sabbath."

O n that day Jesus went out of the house, and was sitting by the sea. And great multitudes gathered to him, so that he got into a boat and sat down, and the whole multitude was standing on the beach. And he spoke many things to them in parables, saying, "Behold, the sower went out to sow; and as he sowed, some seeds fell beside the road, and the birds came and ate them up. And others fell upon the rocky places, where they did not have much soil; and immediately they sprang up, because they had no depth of soil. But when the sun had risen, they were scorched; and because they had no root, they withered away. And others fell among the thorns, and the thorns came up and choked them out. And others fell on the good soil, and yielded a crop, some a hundred-fold, some sixty, and some thirty. He who has ears, let him hear."

nd the disciples came and said to him, "Why do you speak to them in parables?" And he answered and said to them, "To you it has been granted to know the mysteries of the kingdom of heaven, but to them it has not been granted. For whoever has, to him shall more be given, and he shall have an abundance; but whoever does not have, even what he has shall be taken away from him. Therefore I speak to them in parables; because while seeing they do not see, and while hearing they do not hear, nor do they understand. And in their case the prophecy of Isaiah is being fulfilled, which says, 'You will keep on hearing, but will not understand, and you will keep on seeing, but will not perceive; for the heart of this people has become dull, and with their ears they scarcely hear, and they have closed their eyes, lest they should see with their eyes, and hear with their ears, and understand with their heart and return, and I should heal them.' But blessed are your eyes, because they see; and your ears, because they hear. For truly I say to you, that many prophets and righteous men

desired to see what you see, and did not see it; and to hear what you hear, and did not hear it."

 ear then the parable of the sower. When anyone hears the word of the kingdom, and does not understand it, the evil one comes and snatches away what has been sown in his heart. This is the one on whom seed was sown beside the road. And the one on whom seed was sown on the rocky places, this is the man who hears the word and immediately receives it with joy; yet he has no firm root in himself, but is only temporary, and when affliction or persecution arises because of the word, immediately he falls away. And the one on whom the seed was sown among the thorns, this is the man who hears the word, and the worry of the world, and the deceitfulness of riches choke the word, and it becomes unfruitful. And the one on whom seed was sown on the good soil, this is the man who hears the word and understands it; who indeed bears fruit, and brings forth, some a hundredfold, some sixty, and some thirty."

ou will know them by their fruits. Grapes are not gathered from thorn bushes, nor figs from thistles, are they?

There is nothing outside the man which going into him can defile him; but the things which proceed out of the man are what defile the man.

he was saying, "The kingdom of God is like a man who casts seed upon the soil; and goes to bed at night and gets up by day, and the seed sprouts up and grows—how, he himself does not know. The soil produces crops by itself: first the blade, then the head, then the mature grain in the head. But when the crop permits, he immediately puts in the sickle, because the harvest has come."

nd he said; "How shall we picture the kingdom of God, or by what parable shall we present it? It is like a mustard seed, which, when sown upon the soil, though it is smaller than all the seeds that are upon the soil, yet when it is sown, grows up and becomes larger than all the garden plants and forms large branches; so that the birds of the air can nest under its shade.

ow no one after lighting a lamp covers it over with a container, or puts it under a bed; instead he puts it on a lampstand, in order that those who come in may see the light. For nothing is hidden that shall not become evident, nor anything secret that shall not be known and come to light. Therefore take care how you listen; for whoever has, to him shall more be given; and whoever does not have, even what he thinks he has shall be taken away from him."

gain, the kingdom of heaven is like unto a treasure hid in a field; the which when a man hath found, he hideth, and for joy thereof goeth and selleth all that he hath, and buyeth that field.

gain, the kingdom of heaven is like unto a merchant man, seeking goodly pearls, who, when he had found one pearl of great price, went and sold all that he had and bought it.

gain, the kingdom of heaven is like unto a net, that was cast into the sea, and gathered of every kind, which when it was full, they drew to shore, and sat down, and gathered the good into vessels, but cast the bad away. So shall it be at the end of the world: the angels shall come forth, and sever the wicked from among the just, and shall cast them into the furnace of fire; there shall be wailing and gnashing of teeth."

esus saith unto them, "Have ye understood all these things?" They say unto him, "Yea, Lord." But Jesus said unto them, "A prophet is not without honor, save in his own country, and in his own house." And he did not many mighty works there because of their unbelief.

And the Pharisees and some of the scribes gathered together around him when they had come from Jerusalem, and had seen that some of his disciples were eating their bread with impure hands, that is, unwashed. And the Pharisees and the scribes asked him, "Why do your disciples not walk according to the tradition of the elders, but eat their bread with impure hands?" And he said to them, "Rightly did Isaiah prophesy of you hypocrites, as it is written, 'This people honors Me with their lips, but their heart is far away from Me. But in vain do they worship Me, teaching as doctrines the precepts of men.' Neglecting the commandment of God, you hold to the tradition of men."

And after he called the multitude to him again, he began saying to them, "Listen to me all of you, and understand; there is nothing outside the man which going into him can defile him; but the things which proceed out of the man are what defile the man. If any man has ears to hear, let him hear."

esus said, "Neither do I condemn you; go your way. From now on sin no more."

has been caught in adultery, in the very act. Now in the Law, Moses commanded us to stone such women: what then do you say?" And they were saying this, testing him, in order that they might have grounds for accusing him. But Jesus stooped down, and with his finger wrote on the ground. But when they persisted in asking him, he straightened up, and said to them, "He who is without sin among you, let him be the first to throw a stone at her." And again he stooped down and wrote on the ground. And when they heard it, they began to go out one by one, beginning with the older ones, and he was left alone, and the woman, where she had been, in the midst. And straightening up, Jesus said to her, "Woman, where are they? Did no one condemn you?" And she said, "No one, Lord." And

Jesus went to the Mount of Olives. And early in the morning he came again into the temple, and all the people were coming to him. And the scribes and Pharisees brought a woman caught in adultery, and having set her in the midst, they said to him, "Teacher, this woman

Jesus said, "Neither do I condemn you; go your way. From now on sin no more."

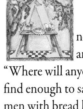

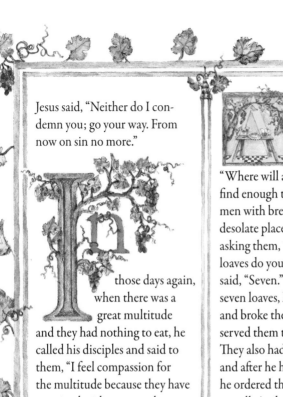

In those days again, when there was a great multitude and they had nothing to eat, he called his disciples and said to them, "I feel compassion for the multitude because they have remained with me now three days, and have nothing to eat; and if I send them away hungry to their home, they will faint on the way; and some of them come from a distance."

nd his disciples answered him, "Where will anyone be able to find enough to satisfy these men with bread here in a desolate place? And he was asking them, "How many loaves do you have?" And they said, "Seven." And taking the seven loaves, he gave thanks and broke them, and they served them to the multitude. They also had a few small fish, and after he had blessed them, he ordered these to be served as well. And they ate and were satisfied; and they picked up seven large baskets full of what was left over of the broken pieces. And about four thousand were there; and he sent them away. And immediately he entered the boat with his disciples, and came to the district of Dalmanutha.

The Pharisees also with the Sadducees came, and tempting desired him that he would shew them a sign from heaven. He answered and said unto them, "When it is evening, ye say, 'It will be fair weather, for the sky is red.' And in the morning, 'It will be foul weather today, for the sky is red and lowering.' O ye hypocrites, ye can discern the face of the sky; but can ye not discern the signs of the times?" And he left them, and departed.

And when his disciples were come to the other side, they had forgotten to take bread. Then Jesus said unto them, "Take heed and beware of the leaven of the Pharisees and of the Sadducees." And they reasoned among themselves, saying, "It is because we have taken no bread." Which when Jesus perceived, he said unto them, "O ye of little faith, why reason among yourselves, because ye have brought no bread? Do ye not yet understand, neither remember the five loaves of the five thousand, and how many baskets ye took up? Neither the seven loaves of the four thousand, and how many baskets ye took up? How is it that ye do not understand that I spake it not to you concerning bread, that ye should beware of the leaven of the Pharisees and of the Sadducees?"

And it came about that while he was praying alone, the disciples were with him, and he questioned them saying, "Who do the multitudes say that I am?" And they answered and said, "John the Baptist, and others say Elijah; but others, that one of the prophets has risen again." And he said to them, "But who do you say that I am?" And Peter answered and said, "The Christ of God." But he warned them, and instructed them not to tell this to anyone, saying "The Son of man must suffer many things, and be rejected by the elders and chief priests and scribes, and be killed, and be raised up on the third day." And he was saying to them all, "If anyone wishes to come after me, let him deny himself, and take up his cross daily, and follow me. For whoever wishes to save his life shall lose it, but whoever loses his life for my sake, he is the one who will save it. For what is a man profited if he gains the whole world, and loses or forfeits himself? For whoever is ashamed of me and my words, of him will the Son of man be ashamed when he comes in his glory, and the glory of the Father and of the holy angels. But I say to you truthfully, there are some of those standing here who shall not taste death until they see the kingdom of God."

 nd there came to him a certain man, who knelt before him and said, "Lord, have mercy on my son, for he is a lunatic. And I brought him to your disciples, and they could not cure him." Then Jesus answered and said, "O faithless and perverse generation, how long shall I be with you? How long shall I suffer you? Bring him hither to me." And Jesus rebuked the devil; and the child was cured from that very hour. Then came the disciples to Jesus apart, and said, "Why could not we cast him out?" And Jesus said unto them, "Because of your unbelief: for verily I say unto you: If ye have faith as a grain of mustard seed, ye shall say unto this mountain, 'Remove hence to yonder place, and it shall remove' and nothing shall be impossible unto you."

 nd they came to Capernaum, and when he was in the house, he began to question them, "What were you discussing on the way?" But they kept silent, for on the way they had discussed with one another which of them was the greatest. And sitting down, he called the twelve and said to them, "If anyone wants to be first, he shall be last of all, and servant of all." And taking a child, he set him before them, and taking him in his arms, he said to them, "Whoever accepts a child like one of these in my name, accepts me; and he who accepts me accepts not me but Him who sent me."

At the same time came the disciples unto Jesus, saying "Who is greatest in the kingdom of heaven?" And Jesus called a little child unto him, and set him in the midst of them and said, "Verily I say unto you: Except ye be converted, and become as little children, ye shall not enter into the kingdom of heaven. And whoso shall receive one such little child in my name receiveth me. Whosoever therefore shall humble himself as this little child, the same is greatest in the kingdom of heaven. But whoso shall offend one of these little ones which believe in me, it were better for him that a millstone were hanged about his neck, and that he were drowned in the depth of the sea."

Woe unto the world because of offences! For it must needs be that offences come; but woe

For what shall it profit a man, if he shall gain the whole world, and lose his own soul?

This people
honoureth me
with their lips,
but their heart is
far away from
me. But in vain
do they worship me,
teaching as doctrines
the precepts of men.

unto you, that in heaven their angels do always behold the face of my Father which is in heaven. For the Son of man is come to save that which was lost. How think ye? If a man have an hundred sheep, and one of them goes astray, doth he not leave the ninety and nine, and goeth into the mountains, and seeketh that which is gone astray? And if so be that he find it, verily I say unto you, he rejoiceth more of that sheep, than of the ninety and nine which went not astray. Even so it is not the will of your Father which is in heaven, that one of these little ones should perish. "Moreover if thy brother shall trespass against thee, go and tell him his fault between thee and him alone; if he shall hear thee, thou hast gained thy brother. But if he will not hear thee, then take with thee one

to that man by whom the offence cometh! Wherefore if thy hand or foot offend thee, cut them off, and cast them from thee; it is better for thee to enter into life halt or maimed, rather than having two hands or two feet to be cast into everlasting fire. And if thine eye offend thee, pluck it out, and cast it from thee; it is better for thee to enter into life with one eye, rather than having two eyes to be cast into hell fire. "Take heed that ye despise not one of these little ones; for I say

or two more, that in the mouth of two or three witnesses every word may be established. And if he shall neglect to hear them, tell it unto the church; but if he neglect to hear the church, let him be unto thee as an heathen man and a publican.

Verily I say unto you, whatsoever ye shall bind on earth shall be bound in heaven and whatsoever ye shall loose on earth shall be loosed in heaven. Again I say unto you, that if two of you shall agree on earth as touching any thing that they shall ask, it shall be done for them of my Father which is in heaven. For where two or three are gathered together in my name, there am I in the midst of them."

Then Peter came and said to him, "Lord, how often shall my brother sin against me and I forgive him? Up to seven times?"
Jesus said to him, "I do not say to you, up to seven times, but up to seventy times seven. For this reason the kingdom of heaven may be compared to a certain king who wished to settle accounts with his slaves. And when he had begun to settle them, there was brought to him one who owed him ten thousand talents. But since he did not have the means to repay, his lord commanded him to be sold, along with his wife and children and all that he had, and repayment to be made. The slave therefore falling

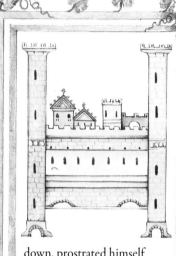

began to entreat him, saying, 'Have patience with me and I will repay you.'

 e was unwilling however, but went and threw him in prison until he should pay back what was owed. So when his fellow slaves saw what had happened they were deeply grieved and came and reported to their lord all that had happened. Then summoning him, his lord said to him, 'You wicked slave, I forgave you all that debt because you entreated me. Should you not also have had mercy on your fellow slave, even as I had mercy on you?' And his lord, moved with anger, handed him over

down, prostrated himself before him, saying, 'Have patience with me, and I will repay you everything.' And the lord of that slave felt compassion and released him and forgave him the debt. But that slave went out and found one of his fellow slaves who owed him a hundred denarii; and he seized him and began to choke him, saying, 'Pay back what you owe.' So his fellow slave fell down and

to the torturers until he should repay all that was owed him. So shall my heavenly Father also do to you, if each of you does not forgive his brother from your heart."

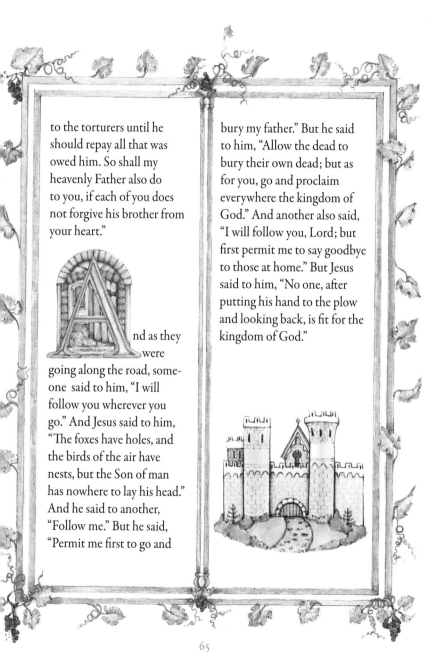

And as they were going along the road, someone said to him, "I will follow you wherever you go." And Jesus said to him, "The foxes have holes, and the birds of the air have nests, but the Son of man has nowhere to lay his head." And he said to another, "Follow me." But he said, "Permit me first to go and bury my father." But he said to him, "Allow the dead to bury their own dead; but as for you, go and proclaim everywhere the kingdom of God." And another also said, "I will follow you, Lord; but first permit me to say goodbye to those at home." But Jesus said to him, "No one, after putting his hand to the plow and looking back, is fit for the kingdom of God."

The foxes have holes, and the birds of the air have nests, but the Son of man has nowhere to lay his head.-

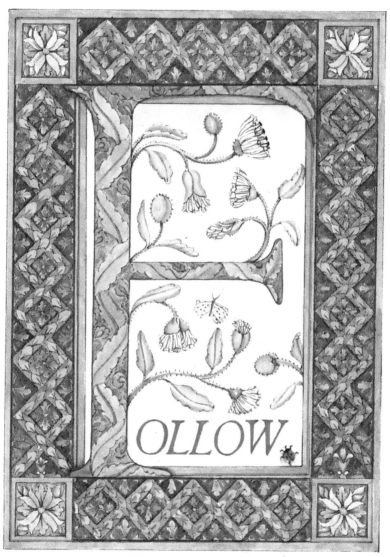

FOLLOW

M E

If you abide in me, and my words abide in you, ask whatever you wish, and it shall be done for you. By this is my Father glorified, that you bear much fruit, and so prove to be my disciples. Just as the Father has loved me, I have also loved you; abide in my love."

"Y ou shall love the Lord your God with all your heart, and with all your soul, and with all your strength, and with all your mind; and your neighbor as yourself."

NOW after this, Jesus chose seventy more to send out before him. "The harvest is plentiful, but the laborers are few." And behold, a certain lawyer stood up and put him to the test, saying, "Teacher, what shall I do to inherit eternal life?" And he said to him, "What is written in the Law? How does it read to you?" And he answered and said, "You shall love the Lord your God with all your heart, and with all your soul, and with all your strength, and with all your mind; and your neighbor as yourself." And he said to him, "You have answered correctly; Do this and you will live." But wishing to justify himself, he said to Jesus, "And who is my neighbor?"

Jesus replied and said, "A certain man was going down from Jerusalem to Jericho; and he fell among robbers, and they stripped him and beat him, and went off leaving him half dead. And by chance a certain priest was going down on that road, and when he saw him, he passed by on the other side. And likewise a Levite also, when he came to the place and saw him, passed by on the other side. But a certain Samaritan, who was on a journey, came upon him; and when he saw him, he felt compassion, and came to him, and bandaged up his wounds, pouring oil and wine on them, and he put him on his own beast, and brought him to an inn, and took care of him. And on the next day he took out two denarii and gave them to the innkeeper and said, 'Take care of him; and whatever more you spend, when I return, I will repay you.' Which of these three do you think proved to be a neighbor to the man who fell into the robbers' hands?" And he said, "The one who showed mercy toward him." And Jesus said to him, "Go and do the same."

Any kingdom divided against itself is laid waste; and a house divided against itself falls. And if Satan also is divided against himself, how shall his kingdom stand? "When a strong man, fully armed, guards his own homestead, his possessions are undisturbed; but when someone stronger than he attacks him and overpowers him, he takes away from him all his armor on which he had relied, and distributes his plunder.

"He who is not with me is against me; and he who does not gather with me, scatters. When the unclean spirit goes out of a man, it passes through waterless places seeking rest, and not finding any, it says, 'I will return to my house from which I came.' And when it comes, it finds it swept and put in order. Then it goes and takes along seven other spirits more evil than itself, and they go in and live there; and the last state of that man becomes worse than the first."

nd everyone who will speak a word against the Son of man, it shall be forgiven him; but he who blasphemes against the Holy Spirit, it shall not be forgiven him. And when they bring you before the synagogues and the rulers and the authorities, do not become anxious about how or what you should speak in your defense, or what you should say; for the Holy Spirit will teach you in that very hour what you ought to say."

nd someone in the crowd said to him, "Teacher, tell my brother to divide the family inheritance with me." But he said to him, "Man, who appointed me a judge or arbiter over you?" And he said to them, "Beware, and be on your guard against every form of greed; for not even when one has an abundance does his life consist of his possessions.

"And do not seek what you shall eat, and what you shall drink, and do not keep worrying. For all these things the nations of the world eagerly seek; but your Father knows that you need these things. But seek for His kingdom, and these things shall be added to you. Fear not, little flock, for it is

your Father's good pleasure to give you the kingdom. "Sell your possessions and give to charity; make yourselves purses which do not wear out, an unfailing treasure in heaven, where no thief comes near, nor moth destroys. For where your treasure is, there will your heart be also."

e dressed in readiness, and keep your lamps alight. And from everyone who has been given much shall much be required; and to whom they entrusted much, of him they will ask all the more."

And he was passing through from one city and village to another, teaching, and proceeding on his way to Jerusalem. And someone said to him, "Lord, are there just a few who are being saved?" And he said to them, "Strive to enter by the narrow door; for many, I tell you, will seek to enter and will not be able. Once the head of the house gets up and shuts the door, and you begin to stand outside and knock on the door, saying, 'Lord, open up to us!' then he will answer and say to you, 'I do not know where you are from.' Then you will begin to say, 'We ate and drank in your presence, and you taught in our streets'; and he will say, 'I tell you, I do not know where you are from; depart from me, all you evildoers.' There will be weeping and gnashing of teeth there when you see Abraham and Isaac and Jacob and all the prophets in the kingdom of God, but yourselves being cast out. And they will come from east and west, and from north and south, and will recline at the table in the kingdom of God. And behold, some are last who will be first and some first who will be last."

Just at that time some Pharisees came up, saying to him, "Go away and depart from here, for Herod wants to kill you." And he said to them, "Go and tell that fox, 'Behold, I cast out demons and perform cures today and tomorrow, and the third day I reach my goal.' Nevertheless I must journey on today and tomorrow and the next day; for it cannot be that a prophet should perish outside of Jerusalem."

Now great multitudes were going along with him, and he turned and said to them, "Whoever does not carry his own cross and come after me cannot be my disciple. For which one of you, when he wants to build a tower, does not first sit down and calculate the cost, to see if he has enough to complete it? Otherwise, when he has laid a foundation, and is not able to finish, all who observe it begin to ridicule him, saying, 'This man began to build and was not able to finish.'

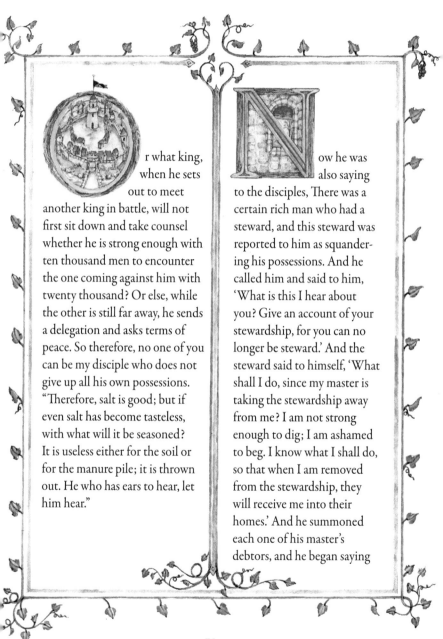

r what king, when he sets out to meet another king in battle, will not first sit down and take counsel whether he is strong enough with ten thousand men to encounter the one coming against him with twenty thousand? Or else, while the other is still far away, he sends a delegation and asks terms of peace. So therefore, no one of you can be my disciple who does not give up all his own possessions. "Therefore, salt is good; but if even salt has become tasteless, with what will it be seasoned? It is useless either for the soil or for the manure pile; it is thrown out. He who has ears to hear, let him hear."

Now he was also saying to the disciples, There was a certain rich man who had a steward, and this steward was reported to him as squandering his possessions. And he called him and said to him, 'What is this I hear about you? Give an account of your stewardship, for you can no longer be steward.' And the steward said to himself, 'What shall I do, since my master is taking the stewardship away from me? I am not strong enough to dig; I am ashamed to beg. I know what I shall do, so that when I am removed from the stewardship, they will receive me into their homes.' And he summoned each one of his master's debtors, and he began saying to the first, 'How much do you owe my master?' And he said, 'A hundred measures of oil.' And he said to him, 'Take your bill, and sit down quickly and write fifty.' Then he said to another, 'And how much do you owe?' And he said, 'A hundred measures of wheat.' And he said to him, 'Take your bill, and write eighty.' "And his master praised the unrighteous steward because he had acted shrewdly; for the sons of this age are more shrewd in relation to their own kind than the sons of light. And I say to you, make friends for yourselves by means of the mammon of unrighteousness; that when it fails, they may receive you into the eternal dwellings. He who is faithful in a very little thing is faithful also in much; and he who is

unrighteous in a very little thing is unrighteous also in much. If therefore you have not been faithful in the use of unrighteous mammon, who will entrust the true riches to you? And if you have not been faithful in the use of that which is another's, who will give you that which is your own? No servant can serve two masters; for either he will hate the one, and love the other, or else he will hold to one, and despise the other. You cannot serve God and mammon."

ow there was a certain rich man, and he habitually dressed in purple and fine linen, gaily living in splendor every day. And a certain poor man named Lazarus was laid at his gate, covered with sores, and longing to be fed with the crumbs which were falling from the rich man's table; besides, even the dogs were coming and licking his sores.

ow it came about that the poor man died and he was carried away by the angels to Abraham's bosom; and the rich man also died and was buried. And in Hades he lifted up his eyes, being in torment and saw Abraham far away, and Lazarus in his bosom. And he cried out and said, 'Father Abraham, have mercy on me, and send Lazarus, that he may dip the tip of his finger in water and cool off my tongue; for I am in agony in this flame.' But Abraham said, 'Child, remember that during your life you received your good things, and likewise Lazarus bad things; but now he is being comforted here, and you are in agony. And besides all this, between us and you there is a great chasm fixed, in order that those who wish to come over from here to you may not be able, and that none may cross over from there to us.'

A new commandment
I give unto you,
That ye love
one another;
as I have loved
you, that ye also
love one another.

Peace I leave with you,
my peace I give unto you:
not as the world giveth,
give I unto you.
Let not your heart
be troubled, neither
let it be afraid.

And he said, 'Then I beg you, Father, that you send him to my father's house–for I have five brothers–that he may warn them, lest they also come to this place of torment.' But Abraham said, 'They have Moses and the Prophets; let them hear them.' But he said, 'No, Father Abraham, but if someone goes to them from the dead they will repent!' But he said to him, 'If they do not listen to Moses and the Prophets, neither will they be persuaded if someone rises from the dead.' "

nd he also told this parable to certain ones who trusted in themselves that they were righteous, and viewed others with contempt: "Two men went up into the temple to pray, one a Pharisee, and the other a tax-gatherer. The Pharisee stood and was praying thus to himself, 'God, I thank Thee that I am not like other people: swindlers, unjust, adulterers, or even like this tax-gatherer. I fast twice a week; I pay tithes of all that I get.' But the tax-gatherer, standing some distance away, was even unwilling to lift up his eyes to heaven, but was beating his breast, saying, 'God, be merciful to me, the sinner!' I tell you, this man went down to his house justified rather than the other; for everyone who exalts himself shall be humbled, but he who humbles himself shall be exalted."

ow having been questioned by the Pharisees as to when the kingdom of God was coming, he answered them and said, "The kingdom of God is not coming with signs to be observed; nor will they say, 'Look, here it is!' or, 'There it is!' For behold, the kingdom of God is in your midst."

And it came about that when Jesus had finished these words, he departed from Galilee, and came into the region of Judea beyond the Jordan; and great multitudes followed him, and he healed them there.

And some Pharisees came to him, testing him, and saying, "Is it lawful for a man to divorce his wife for any cause at all?" And he answered and said, "Have you not read, that He who created them, from the beginning made them male and female, and said 'For this cause a man shall leave his father and mother, and shall cleave to his wife; and the two shall become one flesh'? Consequently they are no longer two, but one flesh. What therefore God has joined together, let no man separate." They said to him, "Why then did Moses command to give her a certificate and divorce her?" He said to them, "Because of your hardness of heart, Moses permitted you to divorce your wives; but from the beginning it has not been this way. And I say to you, whoever divorces his wife, except for immorality, and marries another woman commits adultery." The disciples said to him, "If the relationship of the man with his wife is like this, it is better not to marry." But he said to them, "Not all men can accept this statement, but only those to whom it has been given."

And they were bringing children to him so that he might touch them; and the disciples rebuked them. But when Jesus saw this, he was indignant and said to them, "Permit the children to come to me; do not hinder them; for the kingdom of God belongs to such as these. Truly I say to you, whoever does not receive the kingdom of God like a child shall not enter it at all." And he took them in his arms and began blessing them, laying his hands upon them.

T he thief cometh not, but for to steal, and to kill, and to destroy; I am come that they might have life, and that they might have it more abundantly. I am the good shepherd; the good shepherd giveth his life for the sheep. If I do not the works of my Father, believe me not. But if I do, though ye believe not me, believe the works; that ye may know, and believe, that the Father is in me, and I in Him."

nd, behold, one came and said unto him, "Good Master, what good thing shall I do, that I may have eternal life?" And he said unto him, "Why callest thou me good? There is none good but one, that is, God. But if thou wilt enter into life, keep the commandments." He saith unto him, "Which?" Jesus said, "Thou shalt do no murder, thou shalt not commit adultery, thou shalt not steal, thou shalt not bear false witness, honour thy father and thy mother, and, thou shalt love thy neighbor as thyself." The young man saith unto him, "All these things have I kept from my youth up. What lack I yet?" Jesus said unto him, "If thou wilt be perfect go and sell that thou hast, and give to the poor, and thou shalt have treasure in heaven; and come and follow me." But when the young man heard that saying, he went away sorrowful; for he had great possessions. Then said Jesus to his disciples, "Verily I say unto you, that a rich man shall hardly enter into the kingdom of heaven. And again I say unto you, it is easier for a camel to go through the eye of a needle, than for a rich man to enter the kingdom of God." When his disciples heard it, they were exceedingly amazed, saying, "Who then can be saved?" But Jesus beheld them, and said unto them, "With men this is impossible; but with God all things are possible."

W ITH GOD

all things are possible."

W hile they were on the road, going up to Jerusalem, Jesus was walking on ahead of them; and they were amazed, and those who followed were fearful. And again he took the twelve aside and began to tell them what was going to happen to him, saying, "Behold, we are going up to Jerusalem, and the Son of man will be delivered to the chief

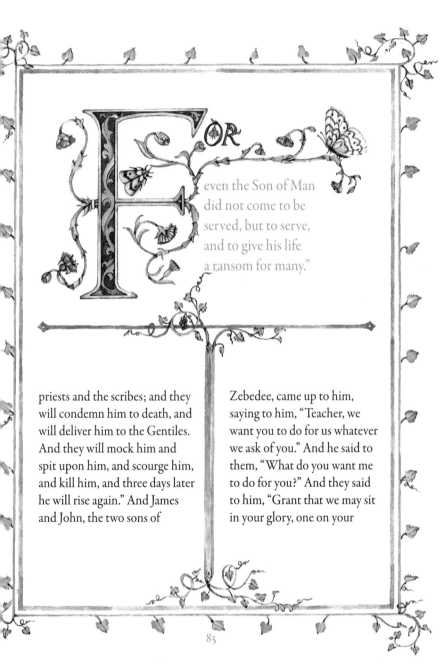

"OR even the Son of Man did not come to be served, but to serve, and to give his life a ransom for many."

priests and the scribes; and they will condemn him to death, and will deliver him to the Gentiles. And they will mock him and spit upon him, and scourge him, and kill him, and three days later he will rise again." And James and John, the two sons of Zebedee, came up to him, saying to him, "Teacher, we want you to do for us whatever we ask of you." And he said to them, "What do you want me to do for you?" And they said to him, "Grant that we may sit in your glory, one on your

Truly, truly, I say to you, unless a grain of wheat falls into the earth and dies, it remains by itself alone; but if it dies, it bears rich fruit."

right, and one on your left." But Jesus said to them; You do not know what you are asking for. Are you able to drink the cup that I drink, or to be baptized with the baptism with which I am baptized?" And they said to him, "We are able." And Jesus said to them, "The cup that I drink you shall drink; and you shall be baptized with the baptism with which I am baptized. But to sit on my right or on my left, this is not mine to give; but it is for those for whom it has been prepared."

nd hearing this, the ten began to feel indignant with James and John. And calling them to himself, Jesus said to them, "You know that those who are recognized as rulers of the Gentiles lord it over them; and their great men exercise authority over them. But it is not so among you, but whoever wishes to become great among you shall be your servant; and whoever wishes to be first among you shall be slave of all. For even the Son of man did not come to be served, but to serve, and to give his life a ransom for many."

The hour has come for the Son of man to be glorified."

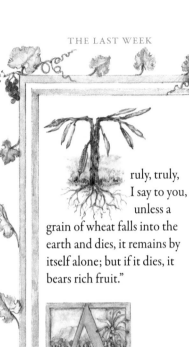

ruly, truly, I say to you, unless a grain of wheat falls into the earth and dies, it remains by itself alone; but if it dies, it bears rich fruit."

nd they came to Jerusalem. And he entered the temple and began to cast out those who were buying and selling in the temple, and overturned the tables of the moneychangers and the seats of those who were selling doves; and he would not permit anyone to carry goods through the temple. "Is it not written, My house shall be called a house of prayer for all the nations? But you have made it a robbers' den." And the chief priests and the scribes heard this, and began seeking how to destroy him; for they were afraid of him, for all the multitude was astonished at his teaching. "Have faith in God. Truly I say to you, whoever says to this mountain, 'Be taken up and cast into the sea,' and does not doubt in his heart, but believes that what he says is going to happen, it shall be granted him. Therefore I say to you, all things for which you pray and ask, believe that you have received them, and they shall be granted you. And whenever you stand praying, forgive, if you have anything against anyone; so that your Father also who is in heaven may forgive you your transgressions. But if you do not forgive, neither will your Father who is in heaven forgive your transgressions."

 e that believeth on me, believeth not on me, but on Him that sent me. And he that seeth me seeth him that sent me. I am come a light into the world, that whosoever believeth on me should not abide in darkness." "And if any man hear my words, and believe not, I judge him not; for I came not to judge the world, but to save the world. He that rejecteth me, and receiveth not my words, hath one that judgeth him; the word that I have spoken, the same shall judge him in the last day. For I have not spoken of myself; but the Father which sent me, he gave me a commandment, what I should say, and what I should speak. And I know that his commandment is life everlasting; whatsoever I speak therefore, even as the Father said unto me, so I speak."

 ear another parable: There was a landowner who planted a vineyard and put a wall around it and dug a winepress in it, and built a tower, and rented it out to vinegrowers, and went on a

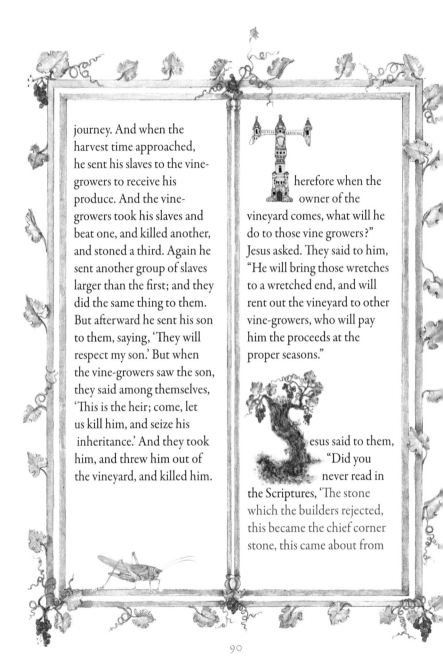

journey. And when the harvest time approached, he sent his slaves to the vine-growers to receive his produce. And the vine-growers took his slaves and beat one, and killed another, and stoned a third. Again he sent another group of slaves larger than the first; and they did the same thing to them. But afterward he sent his son to them, saying, 'They will respect my son.' But when the vine-growers saw the son, they said among themselves, 'This is the heir; come, let us kill him, and seize his inheritance.' And they took him, and threw him out of the vineyard, and killed him.

herefore when the owner of the vineyard comes, what will he do to those vine growers?" Jesus asked. They said to him, "He will bring those wretches to a wretched end, and will rent out the vineyard to other vine-growers, who will pay him the proceeds at the proper seasons."

esus said to them, "Did you never read in the Scriptures, 'The stone which the builders rejected, this became the chief corner stone, this came about from

90

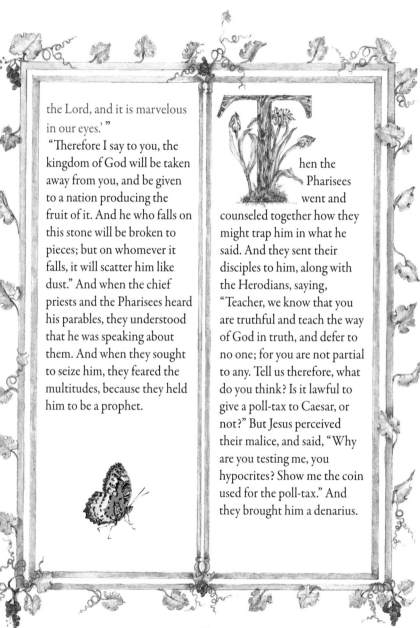

the Lord, and it is marvelous in our eyes.' "

"Therefore I say to you, the kingdom of God will be taken away from you, and be given to a nation producing the fruit of it. And he who falls on this stone will be broken to pieces; but on whomever it falls, it will scatter him like dust." And when the chief priests and the Pharisees heard his parables, they understood that he was speaking about them. And when they sought to seize him, they feared the multitudes, because they held him to be a prophet.

Then the Pharisees went and counseled together how they might trap him in what he said. And they sent their disciples to him, along with the Herodians, saying, "Teacher, we know that you are truthful and teach the way of God in truth, and defer to no one; for you are not partial to any. Tell us therefore, what do you think? Is it lawful to give a poll-tax to Caesar, or not?" But Jesus perceived their malice, and said, "Why are you testing me, you hypocrites? Show me the coin used for the poll-tax." And they brought him a denarius.

And he said to them, "Whose likeness and inscription is this?" They said to him, "Caesar's." Then he said to them, "Then render to Caesar the things that are Caesar's; and to God the things that are God's." And hearing this, they marveled, and leaving him, they went away.

Then one of them, a lawyer, asked him a question, tempting him, and saying "Master, which is the great commandment in the law?" Jesus said unto him, "Thou shalt love the Lord thy God with all thy heart and with all thy soul, and with all thy mind. This is the first and great commandment. And the second is like unto it, Thou shalt love thy neighbor as thyself. On these two commandments hang all the law and the prophets."

And he sat down opposite the treasury, and began observing how the multitude were putting money into the treasury; and many rich people were putting in large sums. And a poor widow came and put in two small copper coins, which amount to a cent. And calling his disciples to him, he said to them, "Truly I say to you, this poor widow put in more than all the contributors to the treasury; for they all put in out of their surplus, but she, out of her poverty, put in all she owned, all she had to live on."

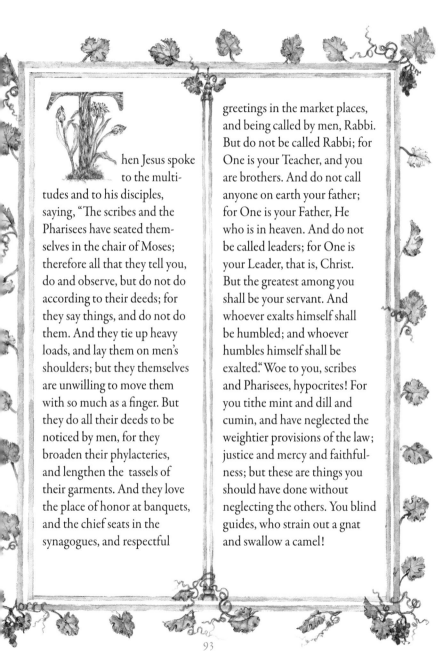

Then Jesus spoke to the multitudes and to his disciples, saying, "The scribes and the Pharisees have seated themselves in the chair of Moses; therefore all that they tell you, do and observe, but do not do according to their deeds; for they say things, and do not do them. And they tie up heavy loads, and lay them on men's shoulders; but they themselves are unwilling to move them with so much as a finger. But they do all their deeds to be noticed by men, for they broaden their phylacteries, and lengthen the tassels of their garments. And they love the place of honor at banquets, and the chief seats in the synagogues, and respectful greetings in the market places, and being called by men, Rabbi. But do not be called Rabbi; for One is your Teacher, and you are brothers. And do not call anyone on earth your father; for One is your Father, He who is in heaven. And do not be called leaders; for One is your Leader, that is, Christ. But the greatest among you shall be your servant. And whoever exalts himself shall be humbled; and whoever humbles himself shall be exalted."Woe to you, scribes and Pharisees, hypocrites! For you tithe mint and dill and cumin, and have neglected the weightier provisions of the law; justice and mercy and faithfulness; but these are things you should have done without neglecting the others. You blind guides, who strain out a gnat and swallow a camel!

"Woe to you, scribes and Pharisees, hypocrites! For you are like whitewashed tombs which on the outside appear beautiful, but inside they are full of dead men's bones and all uncleanness. Even so you too outwardly appear righteous to men, but inwardly you are full of hypocrisy and lawlessness. "Woe to you, scribes and Pharisees, hypocrites! For you build the tombs of the prophets and adorn the monuments of the righteous, and say, 'If we had been living in the days of our fathers, we would not have been partners with them in shedding the blood of the prophets.' Consequently you bear witness against yourselves, that you are sons of those who murdered the prophets. Fill up then the measure of the guilt of your fathers. You serpents, you brood of vipers, how shall you escape the sentence of hell?"

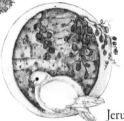

Jerusalem, Jerusalem, who kills the prophets and stones those who are sent to her! How often I wanted to gather your children together, the way a hen gathers her chicks under her wings, and you were unwilling. Behold your house is being left to you desolate! For I say to you, from now on you shall not see me until you say, 'Blessed is he who comes in the name of the Lord!' "

ee to it that no one misleads you. Many will come in my name, saying 'I am he!' and will mislead many. And when you hear of wars and rumors of wars, do not be frightened; those things must take place; but that is not yet the end. For nation will arise against nation, and kingdom against kingdom; there will be earthquakes in various places; there will also be famines. These things are merely the beginning of birth pangs. "For those days will be a time of tribulation such as has not occurred since the beginning of the creation which God created, until now, and never shall. And unless the Lord had shortened those days, no life would have been saved; but for the sake of the elect whom He chose, He shortened the days. And then if anyone says to you, 'Behold, here is the Christ' or 'Behold, he is there,' do not believe him; for false Christs and false prophets will arise, and will show signs and

wonders, in order, if possible, to lead the elect astray. But take heed; behold, I have told you everything in advance.

ut in those days, after that tribulation, the sun will be darkened, and the moon will not give its light, and the stars will be falling from heaven, and the powers that are in the heavens will be shaken. And then they will see the Son of man coming in clouds with great power and glory. And then he will send forth the angels, and will gather together his elect from the four winds, from the farthest end of the earth, to the farthest end of heaven."

LET not your heart be troubled;
ye believe in God,
believe also in me."

In my Father's house are many mansions;
if it were not so, I would have told you.
I go to prepare a place for you."

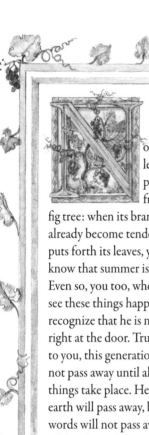

ow learn the parable from the fig tree: when its branch has already become tender, and puts forth its leaves, you know that summer is near. Even so, you too, when you see these things happening, recognize that he is near, right at the door. Truly I say to you, this generation will not pass away until all these things take place. Heaven and earth will pass away, but my words will not pass away. But of that day or hour no one knows, not even the angels in heaven, not the son, but the Father alone. Take heed, keep on the alert, for you do not know when the appointed time is."

For the kingdom of heaven is as a man travelling into a far country, who called his own servants, and delivered unto them his goods. And unto one he gave five talents, to another two, and to another one, to every man according to his several ability and straightway took his journey.

"Then he that had received the five talents went and traded with the same, and made them other five talents. And likewise he that had received two, he also gained other two. But he that had received one went and digged in the earth, and hid his lord's money.

"After a long time the lord of those servants cometh, and

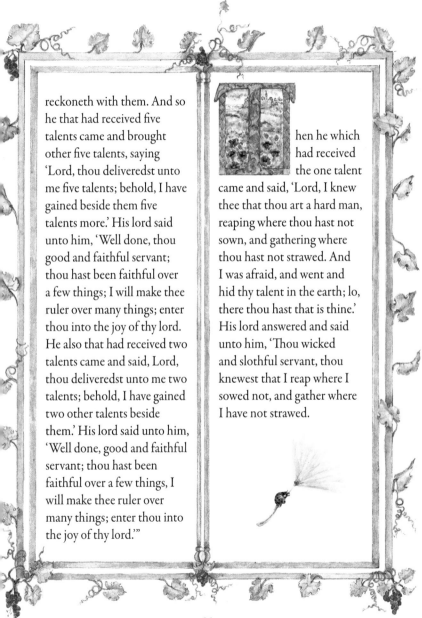

reckoneth with them. And so he that had received five talents came and brought other five talents, saying 'Lord, thou deliveredst unto me five talents; behold, I have gained beside them five talents more.' His lord said unto him, 'Well done, thou good and faithful servant; thou hast been faithful over a few things; I will make thee ruler over many things; enter thou into the joy of thy lord. He also that had received two talents came and said, Lord, thou deliveredst unto me two talents; behold, I have gained two other talents beside them.' His lord said unto him, 'Well done, good and faithful servant; thou hast been faithful over a few things, I will make thee ruler over many things; enter thou into the joy of thy lord.'"

Then he which had received the one talent came and said, 'Lord, I knew thee that thou art a hard man, reaping where thou hast not sown, and gathering where thou hast not strawed. And I was afraid, and went and hid thy talent in the earth; lo, there thou hast that is thine.' His lord answered and said unto him, 'Thou wicked and slothful servant, thou knewest that I reap where I sowed not, and gather where I have not strawed.

 hou oughtest therefore to have put my money to the exchangers, and then at my coming I should have received mine own with usury. Take therefore the talent from him, and give it unto him which hath ten talents.'"

 or unto every one that hath shall be given, and he shall have abundance; but from him that hath not shall be taken away even that which he hath. And cast ye the unprofitable servant into outer darkness; there shall be weeping and gnashing of teeth. When the Son of man shall come in his glory, and all the holy angels with him, then shall he sit upon the throne of his glory. And before him shall be gathered all nations; and he shall separate them one from the other, as a shepherd divideth his sheep from the goats.

 nd he shall set the sheep on his right hand, but the goats on the left. Then shall the King say unto them on his right hand, 'Come, ye blessed of my Father, inherit the kingdom prepared for you from the foundation of the world: for I was an hungered, and ye gave me meat; I was thirsty, and ye gave me drink; I was a stranger, and ye took me in; naked, and ye clothed me; I was sick, and ye visited me; I was in prison, and ye came unto me.'

hen shall the righteous answer him, saying, 'Lord, when saw we thee an hungered, and fed thee? Or thirsty and gave thee drink? When saw we thee a stranger, and took thee in? Or naked, and clothed thee? Or when saw we thee sick, or in prison, and came unto thee?' And the King shall answer and say unto them, 'Verily I say unto you, inasmuch as ye have done it unto one of the least of these my brethren, ye have done it unto me.' "
And it came about that when Jesus had finished all these words, he said to his disciples, "You know that after two days the Passover is coming, and the Son of man is to be delivered up for crucifixion." Then the chief priests and the elders of the people were gathered together in the court of the high priest, named Caiaphas; and they plotted together to seize Jesus by stealth, and kill him. But they were saying, "Not during the festival, lest a riot occur among the people."

nd the day of Passover had come. And when the hour had come he reclined at the table, and the apostles with him. And he said to them, "I have earnestly desired to eat this Passover with you before I suffer; for I say to you, I shall never again eat it until it is fulfilled in the kingdom of God." And when he had taken some bread and given thanks, he broke it, and gave it to them, saying, "This is my body which is given for you; do this in remembrance of me." And in the same way he took the cup after they had eaten, saying, "This cup which is poured out for you is the new covenant in my blood. But behold, the hand of the one betraying me is with me on the table. For indeed, the Son of man is going as it has been determined; but woe to that man by whom he is betrayed!" And they began to discuss among themselves which one of them it might be who was going to do this thing. Then he poured water into the basin, and began to wash the disciples' feet. And so when he had washed their feet, and taken his garments, and reclined at the table again, he said to them, "Do you know what I have done to you? You call me teacher and Lord; and you are right, for so I am. If I then, the Lord and the Teacher, washed your feet, you also ought to wash one another's feet. For I gave you an example that you also should do as I did to you. Truly, truly, I say to you, a slave is not greater than his master; neither is one who is sent greater than the one who sent him. If you know these things, you are blessed if you do them."

And Jesus said, "Truly, truly, I say to you, that one of you will betray me." The disciples began looking at one another, at a loss to know of which one he was speaking. "Lord, who is it?" Jesus therefore answered, "That is the one for whom I shall dip the morsel and give it to him." So when he had dipped the morsel, he took and gave it to Judas, the son of Simon Iscariot.

Let not your hearts be troubled; ye believe in God, believe also in me. In my Father's house are many mansions; if it were not so I would have told you. I go to prepare a place for you. And if I go and prepare a place for you, I will come again, and receive you unto myself; that where I am, there ye may be also. And whither I go ye know, and the way ye know." Thomas saith unto him, "Lord, we know not whither thou goest; and how can we know the way?" Jesus saith unto him,

I am the way, the truth, and the life; no man cometh unto the Father, but by me. If you abide in me, and my words abide in you, ask whatever you wish, and it shall be done for you. By this is my Father glorified, that you bear much fruit, and so prove to be my disciples. Just as the Father has loved me, I have also loved you; abide in my love. If you keep my commandments, you will abide in my love, just as I have kept my Father's commandments, and abide in his love. These things I have spoken to you, that your joy may be made full. This is my commandment, that you love one another, just as I have loved you. Greater love has no one than this, that one lay down his life for his friends.

"A little while and you will not look upon me; and again a little while and you will see me? Truly, truly I tell you that you will weep and mourn, but the world will rejoice. You will have pain, but your pain will turn to joy.

A woman has pain when she is giving birth, when her time has come, but when she has borne her child she no longer remembers her affliction, through joy that a human being has been born into the world. So now you also feel pain; but I will see you again, and your hearts will rejoice, and no one will take that joy away from you."

And after singing a hymn, they went out to the Mount of Olives. Then Jesus said to them, "You will all fall away because of me this night, for it is written, 'I will strike down the shepherd, and the sheep of the flock shall be scattered.' But after I have been raised, I will go before you to Galilee." But Peter answered and said to him, "Even though all may fall away because of you, I will never fall away." Jesus said to him, "Truly I say to you that this very night, before the cock crows, you shall deny me three times."

Then he said to them, "My soul is deeply grieved, to the point of death; remain here and keep watch with me." And he went a little beyond them, and fell on his face and prayed, saying,

"My Father, if it is possible, let this cup pass from me; yet not as I will, but as Thou wilt." And he came to the disciples and found them sleeping, and said to Peter, "So you men could not keep watch with me for one hour? Keep watching and praying, that you may not enter into temptation; the spirit is willing, but the flesh is weak." He went away again a second time and prayed, saying, "My Father, if this cannot pass away unless I drink it, Thy will be done."

And again he came and found them sleeping, for their eyes were heavy. And he left them again, and went away and prayed for a third time, saying the same thing once more. Then he came to the disciples, and said to them, "Are you still sleeping and taking your rest? Behold, the hour is at hand and the Son of man is being betrayed into the hands of sinners. Arise, let us be going; behold, the one who betrays me is at hand!"

When Jesus had spoken these words, he went forth with his disciples over the ravine of the Kidron, where there was a garden, into which he himself entered, and his disciples. Now Judas also, who was betraying him, knew the place; for Jesus had often met there with his disciples. Judas then, having received the Roman cohort, and officers from the chief priests and Pharisees, came there with lanterns and torches and weapons. Now he who was betraying him gave them a sign, saying, "Whomever I shall kiss, he is the one; seize him." And immediately he went to Jesus and said, "Hail Rabbi!" and kissed him. And Jesus said to him "Friend, do what you have come for."

Then they came and laid hands on Jesus and seized him. And behold, one of those who were with Jesus reached and drew out his sword, and struck the slave of the high priest, and cut off his ear. Then Jesus said to him, "Put your sword back into its place; for all those who take up the sword shall perish by the sword." At that time Jesus said, "Have you come out with swords and clubs to arrest me as against a robber? Every day I used to sit in the temple teaching and you did not seize me." Then all the disciples left him and fled.

And having arrested him, they led him away, and brought him to the house of the high priest, but Peter was following at a distance. And after they had kindled a fire in the middle of the courtyard and had sat down together, Peter was sitting among them. And a certain servant girl, seeing him as he sat in the firelight and looking intently at him, said, "This man was with him too." But he denied it, saying, "Woman, I do not know him." And a little later, another saw him and said, "You are one of them too!" But Peter said, "Man, I am not!" And after about an hour had passed, another man began to insist, saying, "Certainly, this man also was with him, for he is a Galilean too." But Peter said, "Man, I do not know what

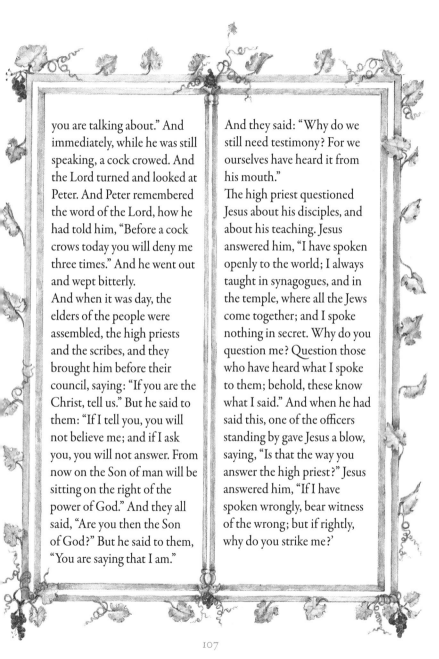

you are talking about." And immediately, while he was still speaking, a cock crowed. And the Lord turned and looked at Peter. And Peter remembered the word of the Lord, how he had told him, "Before a cock crows today you will deny me three times." And he went out and wept bitterly.

And when it was day, the elders of the people were assembled, the high priests and the scribes, and they brought him before their council, saying: "If you are the Christ, tell us." But he said to them: "If I tell you, you will not believe me; and if I ask you, you will not answer. From now on the Son of man will be sitting on the right of the power of God." And they all said, "Are you then the Son of God?" But he said to them, "You are saying that I am."

And they said: "Why do we still need testimony? For we ourselves have heard it from his mouth."

The high priest questioned Jesus about his disciples, and about his teaching. Jesus answered him, "I have spoken openly to the world; I always taught in synagogues, and in the temple, where all the Jews come together; and I spoke nothing in secret. Why do you question me? Question those who have heard what I spoke to them; behold, these know what I said." And when he had said this, one of the officers standing by gave Jesus a blow, saying, "Is that the way you answer the high priest?" Jesus answered him, "If I have spoken wrongly, bear witness of the wrong; but if rightly, why do you strike me?'

But seek ye first the kingdom of God, and his righteousness; and all these things shall be added unto you.

And all things,
whatsoever
ye shall ask in prayer,
believing,
ye shall receive.

And the whole multitude of them arose, and led him unto Pilate. And they began to accuse him, saying, "We found this fellow perverting the nation, and forbidding to give tribute to Caesar, saying that he himself is Christ a King." And Pilate asked him, saying, "Art thou King of the Jews?" And he answered him and said, "Thou sayest it." Then saith Pilate unto him, "Speaketh thou not unto me? Knowest thou not that I have power to crucify thee, and have power to release thee?" Jesus answered, "Thou couldst have no power at all against me, except it were given thee from above; therefore he that delivered me unto thee hath the greater sin." Then said Pilate to the chief priests and to the people, "I find no fault in this man." And Pilate, wanting to release Jesus, addressed them again, but they kept on calling out, saying, "Crucify, crucify him!" And they took Jesus and led him away. And there were also two others, malefactors, led with him to be put to death. And when they were come to the place, which is called Calvary, there they crucified him, and the malefactors, one on the right hand, and the other on the left. Then said Jesus, "Father, forgive them, for they know not what they do." And Pilate wrote an inscription also, and put it

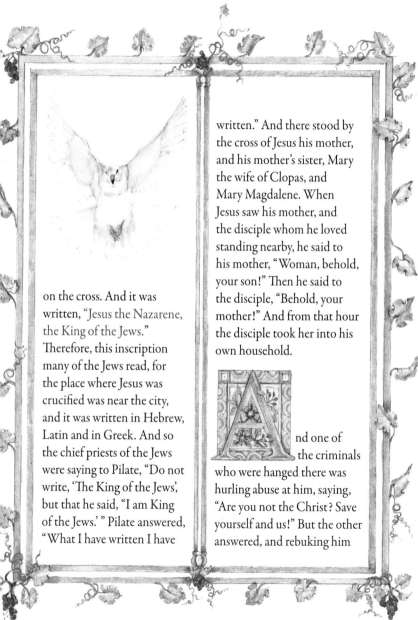

on the cross. And it was written, "Jesus the Nazarene, the King of the Jews." Therefore, this inscription many of the Jews read, for the place where Jesus was crucified was near the city, and it was written in Hebrew, Latin and in Greek. And so the chief priests of the Jews were saying to Pilate, "Do not write, 'The King of the Jews', but that he said, "I am King of the Jews.'" Pilate answered, "What I have written I have written." And there stood by the cross of Jesus his mother, and his mother's sister, Mary the wife of Clopas, and Mary Magdalene. When Jesus saw his mother, and the disciple whom he loved standing nearby, he said to his mother, "Woman, behold, your son!" Then he said to the disciple, "Behold, your mother!" And from that hour the disciple took her into his own household.

And one of the criminals who were hanged there was hurling abuse at him, saying, "Are you not the Christ? Save yourself and us!" But the other answered, and rebuking him said, "Do you not even fear God, since you are under the same sentence of condemnation? And we indeed justly, for we are receiving what we deserve for our deeds; but this man has done nothing wrong." And he was saying, "Lord, remember me when you come into your kingdom!" And he said to him, "Truly I say to you, today you shall be with me in Paradise."

And it was about the sixth hour, and there was a darkness over all the earth until the ninth hour. And about the ninth hour Jesus cried with a loud voice, saying, "Eli, Eli, lama sabachthani?" that is to say, "My God, my God, why hast Thou forsaken me?"

After this Jesus, knowing that all things had already been accomplished, in order that the Scripture might be fulfilled, said, "I am thirsty." A jar full of sour wine was standing there; so they put a sponge full of the sour wine upon a branch of hyssop, and brought it up to his mouth. When Jesus therefore had received the sour wine, he said, "It is finished!" And when Jesus had cried with a loud voice, he said, "Father, into Thy hands I commend my spirit." And having said thus, he gave up the ghost.

Peace

I leave with you; my peace I give to you; not as the world gives, do I give to you. Let not your heart be troubled, nor let it be fearful."

"All power is given unto you in heaven and in earth. Go ye therefore, and teach all nations, baptizing them in the name of the Father, and of the Son, and of the Holy Ghost, teaching them to observe all this whatsoever I have commanded you, and lo, I am with you always, even unto the end of the world.

Amen.

"Heaven and earth will pass away, but my words will not pass away."

I am the vine, ye are the branches: He that abideth in me, and I in him, the same bringeth forth much fruit: for without me ye can do nothing.

Our Father who art in heaven,
Hallowed be thy name.
Thy kingdom come.
Thy will be done
on earth as it is in heaven.
Give us this day our daily bread,
and forgive us our trespasses,
as we forgive those
who trespass against us,
and lead us not into temptation,
but deliver us from evil.
For thine is the kingdom,
and the power, and the glory,
for ever and ever

Amen.

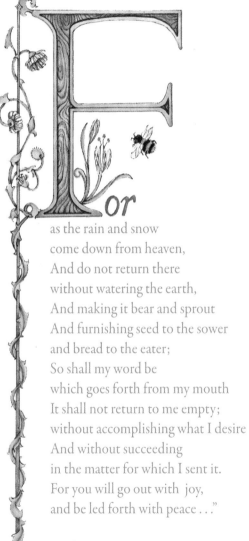

For

as the rain and snow
come down from heaven,
And do not return there
without watering the earth,
And making it bear and sprout
And furnishing seed to the sower
and bread to the eater;
So shall my word be
which goes forth from my mouth
It shall not return to me empty;
without accomplishing what I desire
And without succeeding
in the matter for which I sent it.
For you will go out with joy,
and be led forth with peace . . . "

Isaiah 55:10-12

MUSING & MEDITATIONS